ONE DIRECTION

What Makes You Beautiful

Mary Boone

TRIUMPH
BOOKS

This book is available in quantity at special discounts for your group or organization. For further information, contact:

Triumph Books LLC
814 North Franklin Street
Chicago, Illinois 60610
Phone: (312) 337-0747
www.triumphbooks.com

Printed in U.S.A.

ISBN: 978-1-60078-777-5

Content developed and packaged by Rockett Media, Inc.
Writer: Mary Boone
Editor: Bob Baker
Design and page production Andrew Burwell
Cover design by Andrew Burwell

Photographs courtesy of Getty Images unless otherwise noted

ONE DIRECTION

What Makes You Beautiful

05 CHAPTER 1: FROM X FACTOR TO EXTREMELY HOT

One Direction finished in third place on *The X Factor* in the 2010 U.K. finales. They've used that platform to catapult themselves into the worldwide spotlight.

27 CHAPTER 2: GETTING TO KNOW THE GUYS

From tattoos to a fear of spoons, we tell you everything you need to know about Niall, Zayn, Liam, Harry, and Louis.

49 CHAPTER 3: WILL U.K. FAME TRANSLATE IN THE U.S.?

Not all British musical acts find success on the other side of the pond. What does One Direction have that sets them apart from the rest?

69 CHAPTER 4: BOY BANDS FROM YEARS GONE BY

Boy bands are nothing new – but they are in a class all their own. How do the 1D guys feel about being part of this oft-maligned genre and how are they trying to revamp it?

91 CHAPTER 5: FAN-tastic

One Direction fans are loyal and loud. Several cities have had to shut down streets when the band makes appearances. Here's how some of the group's biggest fans are showing their love.

110 EPILOGUE: WHAT DOES THE FUTURE HOLD?

A North American tour, possible collaborations with Justin Bieber and Big Time Rush ... the future looks bright for One Direction.

CHAPTER ONE
FROM X FACTOR TO EXTREMELY HOT

They were the boys who were not quite good enough to make the cut for a televised talent show in England. They could have packed up and gone home. But, instead, they're touring the world, selling albums at record pace, melting the hearts of young girls, and drawing countless comparisons to a well-known British band from a few years back – The Beatles.

Meet One Direction: five well-coiffed guys, ages 17-20, who only first met in 2010, but who are enjoying a meteoric rise to the top of the charts on both sides of the Atlantic.

Justin who? He's so "last year."

Niall Horan, Zayn Malik, Liam Payne, Harry Styles, and Louis Tomlinson are the names young music fans need to know now.

The guys quite famously got rejected when they auditioned as individuals for the 2010 version of *The X Factor*, a television

SIMON COWELL:

Most Americans know Simon Cowell as the multi-millionaire music mogul who verbally insults contestants on *American Idol* and, more recently *X Factor USA*.

What most viewers don't realize is that Cowell isn't just a high-paid talent show judge. He's also one of the most successful people in the music industry – though he's hardly a musician himself.

In a 2007 interview with Anderson Cooper, which aired on 60 *Minutes*, Cowell quite famously defined his own talent:

Anderson Cooper: "Do you sing?"

Simon Cowell: "No."

COOPER: "Do you play an instrument?"

COWELL: "Guitar, very badly."

COOPER: "Do you read music?"

COWELL: "No."

COOPER: "Do you produce albums?"

COWELL: "No."

COOPER: "So, what actually do you do?"

COWELL: "Guess what's going to be popular."

COOPER: "You guess what's going to be popular?"

COWELL: "Literally, that."

The truth is, he's so good at "guessing" that he owns luxurious homes in London and Beverly Hills and runs successful companies on both sides of the pond. In addition to his successful TV shows, he's a record executive for Sony BMG.

The son of a music industry executive and a socialite/ballet dancer, Cowell got early exposure to the entertainment world. He dropped out of school at age 16 and worked odd jobs until his father got him a job with EMI Music Publishing. He started off doing errands and worked his way up the ladder until he got a job at EMI as a record producer. He eventually left that company to start his own small record labels. He later joined BMG where he helped launch the bands Five and Westlife.

Cowell made his first TV appearance in 2001 as a judge on U.K. talent show *Pop Idol*, which was later adapted in the United States as *American Idol*.

SNARKY AND MORE

Cowell helped make *American Idol* one of the most popular TV shows in the United States. In turn, the show helped make Cowell a celebrity in his own right.

He left *American Idol* in 2009 and has also been a celebrity judge on shows including *The X Factor* and *Britain's Got Talent.*

His Syco label signed the top two finishers of the first season of *Pop Idol*, Will Young and Gareth Gates, both of whom went on score No. 1 hits in the United Kingdom. More recently, his

musical "creations" include the group Il Divo, a multinational operatic pop group that, to date, has sold more than 26 million albums worldwide.

Cowell doesn't consider himself a musician, he prefers the label "entrepreneur." In his 2003 book, *I Don't Mean to be Rude, But ...,* he wrote: "I've always treated the music business as a business. Whether I'm making TV shows or signing artists, you have to do it by the head and not the heart – I run my businesses that way."

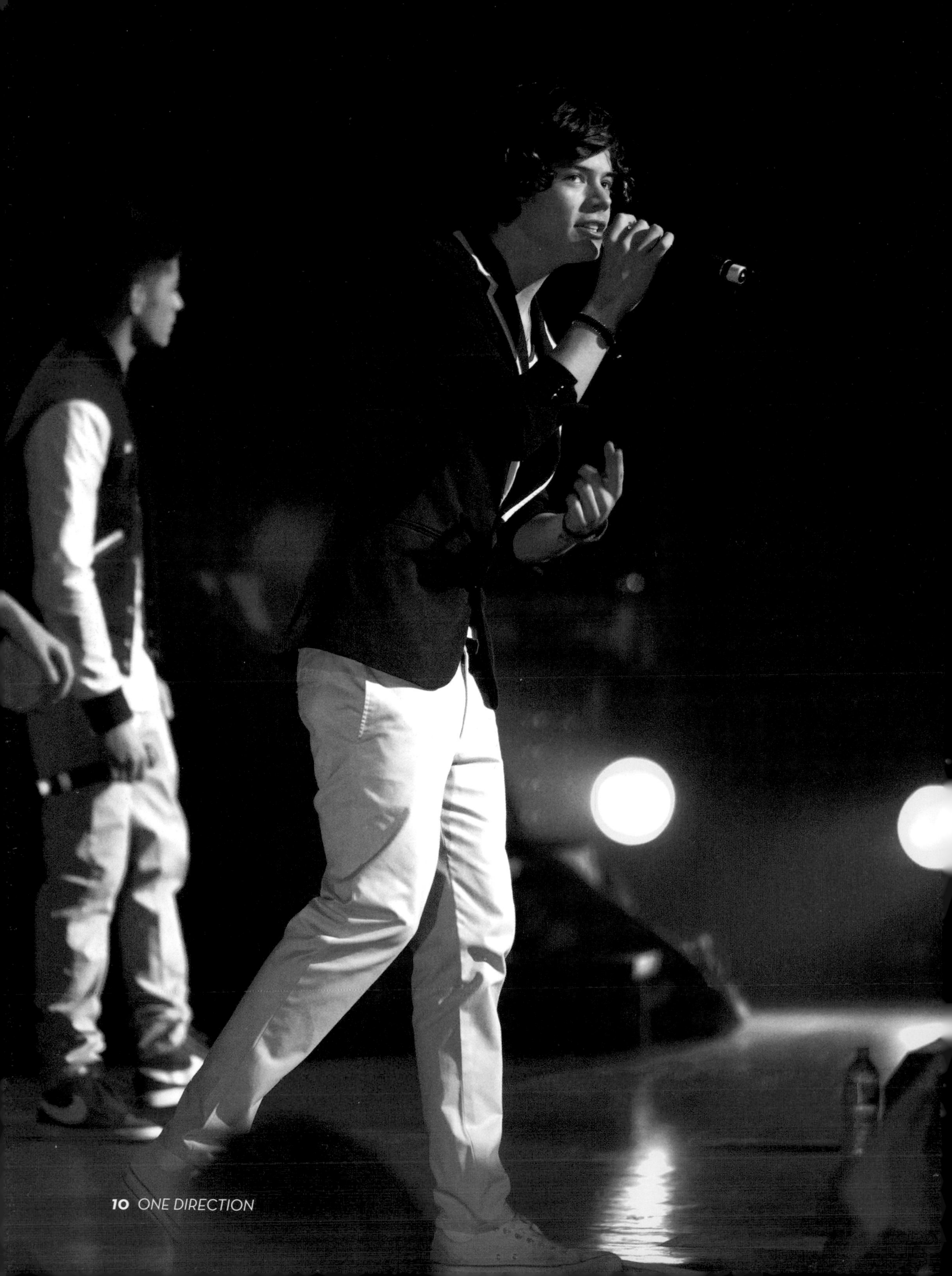

music competition in the United Kingdom. Nicole Scherzinger, a guest judge on the show, stepped in and suggested they form a band, thus qualifying for the contest's "Groups" division.

"It was pretty much a choice of progress in the competition as a group or go home as a solo," Zayn told Australia's Nova FM radio station. They decided to try it out as a group – though it wasn't as easy as you might think.

Liam came into the competition with a bit of experience. He was studying musical technology in college at the time and had once performed for a crowd of more than 26,000 at a soccer match. Two years earlier, he'd also auditioned for *The X Factor,* and made it to the later stage where they perform at the judges' homes.

The other guys, though, had considerably less experience. Louis had taken a few singing lessons and had been in a school production of *Grease.* Harry had performed in a school Battle of the Bands competition. Zayn had appeared in a couple of school musicals, and Niall was in the school choir.

"We didn't know what a harmony was," Zayn said. "We just sang in unison for two weeks."

Liam laughs when he thinks back to those initial meetings and rehearsals. "My first thought was, 'Are we going to make this work when we don't know each other?'

It was such a leap of faith," he said.

"The first few days were quite tough," he told the *South Wales Echo.* "We all had different ideas, but we didn't really know what a group was about."

X FACTOR WINNERS MAKING THEIR OWN MARKS

Singers Matt Cardle and Rebecca Ferguson beat One Direction in the 2010 finale of *The X Factor.* Where are they now? What are they doing?

Cardle, who auditioned for the seventh season of *The X Factor* singing Amy Winehouse's "You Know I'm No Good," came out on top of the talent competition with 44.61 percent of the vote. As the winner, he received a £1 million recording contract (worth approximately 1.6 million U.S. dollars) with Syco Music. Cardle's debut single, "When We Collide," was released immediately after he won. It sold 439,000 copies in its first week.

The former bricklayer and painter's debut album, *Letters,* was released in October 2011, and he's already busy working on the follow-up.

Cardle, who began writing songs when he was just 11 years old, had performed and toured for 14 years but felt he wasn't getting anywhere in the music industry. That's when he reluctantly decided to enter the televised singing competition.

Cardle has a strange relationship with *The X Factor*: he's grateful for the boost it has given his career, but said he was never fully comfortable with the show.

"I feel a bit bad saying that because I don't want people to get the impression that I think I was too good or too cool for *X Factor,*" Cardle told *The Sunday World* (Ireland). "A lot of people see it as a sneaky back door entrance to the music industry and skipping the queue. But I had put in a decade of leg work and ground work and I earned the right to be there. I'm not sure how much young people on the show appreciated it, but I certainly did. Now the public has put me where I am, and I thank them deeply for it."

English singer/songwriter Rebecca Ferguson also edged out One Direction in the 2010 finale of *The X Factor*, claiming the No. 2 spot.

She released her debut single, "Nothing's Real But Love" in November 2011; it entered the U.K. singles chart at No. 10. Her debut album, *Heaven*, was released in December 2011 in the United Kingdom; it was released in the United States in May 2012. The Liverpool-born singer wrote all 10 songs on her first album and signed a deal with EMI Music Publishing.

Ferguson recently completed a sold-out U.K. tour; her 2012 schedule has her performing and making appearances in the United States, Germany, Australia, Switzerland, and New Zealand. She also just became the fifth person ever to duet with U.S. musical legend Lionel Richie during his April 2012 ITV special. Speaking about the honor, Richie said:

"I've only ever sung (the song 'Endless Love') with four women, and I thought Rebecca would be the ideal voice to do it for the fifth time. There's a lot to live up to, but I know she'll be great."

On a more personal note, Ferguson dated One Direction songster Zayn Malik (who's six years younger than she is) for four months back in 2011, but that relationship appears to be over and done with. When a fan at her March 13, 2012, concert at London's Theatre Royal shouted out "Zayn," Ferguson was quick to reply: "That's so last year."

The awkwardness didn't last long. The boys gelled and, with some serious dedication to rehearsal, they were able to sail through the early competition and moved on to the live shows, mentored by *The X Factor* creator, Simon Cowell.

As the guys developed skills and confidence, they quickly attracted a huge fan base. It was an incredible now-or-never kind of experience.

"Normally when you put together a band, they have some time to go away and develop, but we had to do that in a live competition, in front of 20 million people," Liam said. "If you make a mistake in front of an audience like that, you get voted out. We had no room for error whatsoever. We had to grow up very, very fast."

During the show, the contestants all stay together in a house in London, where the One Direction boys quickly earned a reputation as jokesters, making prank telephone calls and impersonating their fellow competitors.

FIVE OTHER REASONS TO LOVE NICOLE

It's no secret that entertainer Nicole Scherzinger played a part in forming One Direction. When the guys failed to get through *The X Factor* auditions as solo artists, it was Scherzinger, a judge on the show, who suggested they form a group.

"I practically put One Direction together with my hands tied behind my back," she joked to *Now Daily* in July 2011.

As if Liam, Louis, Niall, Harry, and Zayn aren't good enough reasons to love this Hawaiian-born singer/dancer/actress/model, we've found five additional reasons to show Nicole some love:

1. The Pussycat Dolls. This group started as a dance-only ensemble back in 1995. Scherzinger joined the group in 2003 and served as lead vocalist during the PCD's evolution into a popular music group. She led the multi-platinum, scantily clad group to 10 million in album sales and numerous sold-out world-wide tours. Never heard of them? Check out their big hit "Don't Cha."

2. She can move. Sure, she danced as part of The Pussycat Dolls but, thanks to *Dancing with the Stars*, she now has the prize to prove her prowess. Scherzinger and her professional dance partner, Derek Hough, won the show's famed mirror ball trophy with their jive to "Proud Mary." She beat out Olympic ice skater Evan Lysacek and ESPN reporter Erin Andrews in the finals of the show's tenth season.

3. **She speaks her mind.** When she was fired from the *X Factor USA* judging panel, show producer Simon Cowell described Scherzinger as having "Daffy Duck's brain" but the beauty of cartoon character Jessica Rabbit. She bit her tongue for a while, but finally struck back in February 2012, saying Simon was simply "afraid" of her. "I know I'm not ditzy like Daffy Duck," she told *Vibe* magazine. "If I seem that way, maybe it's just me being coy. Simon's just afraid of me." Take that, Mr. Cowell!

4. **She can be bad.** Scherzinger is thrilled to have landed a role as villain Lily alongside Will Smith and Tommy Lee Jones in 2012's *Men in Black III.* The singer says the role mirrors the "fun" she has in her musical performances. "On stage I always get into a kind of superhero or super villain role when I'm performing," she told Contactmusic.com. "But super villains are more fun, don't you think? If you're going to take over the world, you might as well have fun with it."

5. **She likes fast cars.** Oh, and the guys who drive them too – more

specifically, her boyfriend is Formula One driver Lewis Hamilton. The two dated for three years before taking a six-month break, then they got back together. The couple is believed to have decided to give their relationship another go at the advice of Lewis' father, Anthony. Talking to the *Daily Star* newspaper, a source explained: "Lewis' dad told him if he wants to win the championship again he needs a settled personal life ... His family thinks there will be a wedding by the end of next year." And Nicole will, most certainly, look gorgeous in white.

Fortunately, they limited their silliness to off-stage moments. When they were competing, the guys were all business. During the 10 weeks of live shows, One Direction covered songs ranging from Bryan Adams' "Summer of '69" and Coldplay's "Viva La Vida" to Kelly Clarkson's "My Life Would Suck Without You" and Snow Patrol's "Chasing Cars," becoming the first-ever manufactured group to make it through the show's first nine weeks of on-air competition.

In the show's final episode, the band performed Elton John's "Your Song," World Party's "She's the One" (with pop superstar Robbie Williams) and Natalie Imbruglia's "Torn."

One Direction didn't end up winning

The X Factor; rather, they finished in third place, behind runner-up Rebecca Ferguson and champion Matt Cardle. It's safe to say the loss has not hampered their career – not in the slightest.

In fact, on March 22, 2012, One Direction became the first U.K. group ever to debut at No. 1 on the U.S. Billboard 200 album chart, a feat they accomplished by knocking megastars Bruce Springsteen and Adele each down a rung.

"When we got put together as a group, we couldn't imagine ourselves coming to America, let alone releasing our album here, so for us to be sitting at the top of the U.S. album charts is unbelievable," Niall said in a statement released by the group's record label.

One Direction sold more than 176,000 copies of its debut album, *Up All Night,* within the first week of its release. The CD shot straight to the top of the digital charts within minutes of its official release on March 13, 2012.

Music insiders may have had the boy band on their radar, but it wasn't until early March 2012, when One Direction made its American television debut, that most folks

began to sit up and take notice. A crowd of more than 10,000 screaming fans – many of them tween- and teenage girls – showed up for the *Today* show taping at Rockefeller Center, prompting NBC to employ security measures usually reserved for superstars like Lady Gaga or Chris Brown.

By mid-March 2012, the band had more than 12 million Twitter followers, 3.6 million Facebook fans, and they'd racked up more than 204 million views on YouTube.

The guys admit they still can't believe

how much their lives have changed in such a short time.

"I think we went into the (*X Factor*) competition just like anyone else who enters – to see how you'll do and not expecting anything really," Zayn said. "My whole reason in the first place was my mum, who used to tell me I could sing, but I wanted to find out from someone else."

When a recent European tour took the group to Dublin, Niall says he couldn't help but get nostalgic about his audition at the city's convention center.

"It's so weird to think that just a year-and-a-half ago, I was there auditioning and now everything is so mad," he said.

While getting that initial rejection from *The X Factor* was a little disheartening, in

retrospect – the subsequent rise to fame has made the experience considerably more tolerable.

"I agree with the decision now," Liam told the *Birmingham (England) Mail* in February 2012. "I was too young. Some things are meant to happen and this is one of those things. I was meant to do it in a band. I have made four new best friends out of it, so I'm happy as Larry."

"Happy as Larry," by the way, is a common British phrase that means really, really happy.

So, it's fair to say, U.S. music fans are "Happy as Larry" with One Direction's rise to stardom. Sometimes five heads really are better than one.

CHAPTER TWO
GETTING TO KNOW THE GUYS

They travel together, they work together, they play together.

In so many ways, One Direction members have morphed into a cohesive group, with their unified effort much more powerful than their singular performances might ever have been. One voice is lovely; five harmonizing voices have girls trembling on both sides of the Atlantic.

As singularly sensational as these guys are, true fans know One Direction's members have diverse backgrounds, upbringings, beliefs, and personalities.

Here's a close-up look at the band's five very different members:

Niall James Horan
Birthdate: September 13, 1993
Astrological sign: Virgo
Hometown: Mullingar in Westmeath, Ireland
On Twitter: @NiallOfficial

NIALL

WHOSE TWEET WAS THAT?

You know their favorite colors, their astrological signs, their hometowns, their reps, and their favorite sports teams. But, do you know One Direction well enough to know which tweet belongs to which of the handsome hotties?

We provide the tweets, you guess the tweeter. Answers follow.

1. Choose your paths carefully because future's uncertain. But that's what makes life exciting, right? (2/11/12)

2. Irish fans. Yo. Yo. Yo. (2/15/12)

3. Really really need some Yorkshire tea on tour. (1/4/12)

4. I was born to stand tall. (2/26/12)

5. Absolutely LOVE the fact @SimonCowell likes Anchorman haha too funny! (12/12/11)

6. Life is full of surprising events, they all happen for a reason though so we may resent! (3/19/12)

7. Life is like a book. just cause one chapter closes doesn't mean the book is over. So live life, and don't skip to the end. (1/15/12)

8. Good morning all. How the bloody hell is everyone? (3/9/12)

9. Eating some of possibly the best tasting pizza I've ever had! Chicago is the place for pizza! And loud fans u guys were amazing (2/24/12)

10. Why does everything seem better when it's in a bottle shaped like a bear? (3/7/12)

11. Stop the tape and rewind. (11/16/11)

12. May your neighbours respect you, trouble neglect you, angels protect you and heaven accept you. (3/8/12)

13. CAPITAL LETTERS ARE VERY LOUDDD!!!!! (3/19/12)

14. Don't ya hate it when your blackberry goes really slow and u feel like punching it in the memory card! (11/29/11)

15. I just got caked in the face...and a cake made of ice cream is harder than regular cake. Hard cake in the face. (3/14/12)

16. @SimonCowell Uncle Simon have you got your copy of Up All Night yet? If you haven't, me and you are gonna fall out, Mr. (3/18/12)

17. Wow this tour bus bed feels like heaven... (1/11/12)

18. You know what? You guys make me so happy, I was just thinking about all the stuff I've got to do over the past year and I can't believe ... (3/18/12)

19. Just watched Spiderman on Broadway, was rather enjoyable. I wouldn't mind one of the suits but they're quite tight...bit risky. (3/15/12)

20. Can't sleep. Still so happy. Thank YOU again for making this possible! (2/21/12)

Answers: 1. Zayn; 2. Liam; 3. Louis; 4. Niall; 5. Louis; 6. Zayn; 7. Niall; 8. Louis; 9. Zayn; 10. Harry; 11. Niall; 12. Zayn; 13. Liam; 14. Zayn; 15. Harry; 16. Liam; 17. Zayn; 18. Liam; 19. Harry; 20. Niall

ZAYN

The basics: Niall is the only Irish member of One Direction; he's also the band's lone blond. He grew up in Mullingar, a town of about 20,000, where his father is a butcher. In addition to being a talented vocalist, Niall plays the guitar. He is a fan of the Irish band Westlife and also Take That and Enz Inc.

His rep: He's the "funny one" of the group. "Niall is happy-go-lucky and out to have a good time. He just loves people," band mate Liam said.

When did he first know he had talent? As a 10-year-old, he was singing in the car. He sounded so good that his aunt thought the radio was on. "Exactly the same thing happened to Michael Bublé with his dad," Niall said. "He's my absolute hero so I like the fact we have a similar story."

What you may not know about him: He had a bad case of "Irish teeth." Prior to heading for the U.S., One Direction managers had him fitted for braces to fix up his now-adorable smile.

Zayn Jawaad Malik

Birthdate: January 12, 1993
Astrological sign: Capricorn
Hometown: West Lane Baildon, Bradford, England
On Twitter: @zaynmalik1D

The basics: Zayn first came to the attention of *The X Factor* audience members when he refused to join other contestants on stage for a dance routine during the boot camp portion of the audition. Simon

HOW MUCH DO YOU KNOW ABOUT ONE DIRECTION?

1. Two band members share the same middle name. Who are they?
2. Which of the musicians tweeted that he has a "fear of spoons"?
3. What is Louis Tomlinson's favorite color?
4. One Direction's first U.S. tour kicked off in what city?
5. One Direction was the musical guest on the April 7, 2012, episode of *Saturday Night Live*. Who was the show's host that night?
6. What is the name of the *iCarly* episode on which One Direction guest starred?
7. Which fellow pop artist is mentioned by name in One Direction's song "Up All Night"?
8. Who is the group's youngest member?
9. One Direction has filmed a series of television commercials for one of their favorite video games. What's the game?
10. Which band member previously performed with a group called White Eskimo?
11. As their qualifying song on *The X Factor*, One Direction performed an acoustic version of what tune?
12. Which organization named One Direction "Worst Band of the Year" at a February 29, 2012, awards ceremony?
13. Which band member suffered from a childhood illness that resulted in kidney damage?
14. Where did the guys film the music video for their single "What Makes You Beautiful"?
15. One of the band members created some of the illustrations for One Direction's debut CD. Who was it?

Answers:

1. Liam and Niall share the middle name "James"
2. Liam Payne
3. Dark red
4. Chicago
5. Sofia Vergara from ABC's TV show *Modern Family*
6. "iGot Jungle Worms"
7. Katy Perry
8. Harry is the youngest; his Feb. 1, 1994, birth date makes him about four and a half months younger than Niall
9. The band members are ambassadors for Nintendo's latest Pokemon releases "Pokemon Black Version" and "Pokemon White Version"
10. Harry
11. "Torn"
12. New Musical Express, popularly known by the initials NME, a weekly U.K. music publication
13. Liam
14. Malibu, California
15. Zayn

Cowell noticed his reluctance to participate and convinced him that by not dancing, he was ruining the opportunity for himself. He returned to the routine and the rest is history. Zayn says if he hadn't auditioned for *The X Factor*, he likely would have gone to college to become a teacher.

His rep: He's laid-back and a little vain. "Zayn is very quiet but also pretty mental and very random," Liam noted.

All inked-up: Zayn is a big fan of body art and has four tattoos: a Japanese symbol which is said to mean "lucky" on his hip; a yin and yang symbol on his wrist; his grandfather's name in Arabic on his chest; and, a hand with fingers crossed for good luck on his arm.

What you may not know about him: He's an artist and received credit for some of the illustrations on the group's debut CD.

Liam James Payne

Birthdate: August 29, 1993
Astrological sign: Virgo
Hometown: Wolverhampton, England
On Twitter: @LiamoPayne

The basics: As a 14-year-old, Liam auditioned for *The X Factor* and made it through to the judges' houses. That time

U.K. SLANG

Fans are hanging on their every word, but sometimes what they say doesn't make complete sense. One Direction's four British and one Irish member tend to use a bit of U.K. slang. Some phrases you may hear the guys say include:

1. **Ace** – Very good
2. **Blow me** – An expression of complete surprise, as in "I am so surprised you could knock me over just by blowing."
3. **Brill** – Short for "brilliant," means awesome or cool.
4. **Cheeky** – Flippant or bold
5. **Full of beans** – To have lots of energy
6. **Give us a bell** – Call me
7. **Gobsmacked** – Amazed
8. **Gormless** – Clueless or lacking intelligence
9. **Horses for courses** – To each his own
10. **Knees-up** – Party that generally includes dancing
11. **Off your trolley** – Behaving in a silly or unusual way
12. **Smashing** – Terrific or impressive
13. **Waffle** – To talk on and on about nothing
14. **Wobbler** – Tantrum or fit
15. **Wonky** – Shaky or unstable
16. **Zonked** – Exhausted or worn out

around, though, judge Simon Cowell told him he was simply too young and advised him to wait a couple years before trying again. Things obviously went his way when he returned to the show in 2010. After being put into One Direction, Liam was often assigned the task of singing lead vocals. He says if he wasn't a singer, he would want to be a firefighter or a gym teacher.

His rep: He's the "smart and sensible" one. "I often get described as Papa Smurf," he said.

If the shoe fits: Liam ended up losing his shoe when the band was mobbed by fans at Paris' Gare De Nord train station. "I got it back afterwards. Some girls brought it back and told me that a homeless man took it off the floor and they had to buy it back off him for 30 euros. I didn't really want to put it back on because I was worried he might have done a little wee in it or something."

What you may not know about him: Liam was born prematurely and had many health challenges as a baby. As a result, he has only one working kidney. "I've still got both kidneys," he said, "but one doesn't

HARRY

work, so I have to be careful not to drink too much, even water, and I have to keep myself as healthy as possible."

Harry Edward Styles
Birthdate: February 1, 1994
Astrological sign: Aquarius
Hometown: Holmes Chapel, Cheshire, England
On Twitter: @Harry_Styles

The basics: Harry, who shares One Direction lead vocal responsibilities with Liam, is the group's youngest member. Prior to auditioning for *The X Factor*, he and three friends had formed a band called White Eskimo. His personal music favs include Foster the People, Coldplay, and Kings of Leon. Harry, who hails from a village with fewer than 5,000 people, is an avid fan of Manchester United.

Older women: Harry made a lot of headlines when, in October 2011, he started dating British TV personality Caroline Flack, who is 15 years his senior. When the pair broke up three months later, Harry went

to Twitter to let fans know the decision to split was mutual: "Please know I didn't 'dump' Caroline. This was a mutual decision. She is one of the kindest, sweetest people I know."

His rep: They're all flirts, but he's the king of the flirts. "Harry is the cheeky little chappy," Liam said. He also has *the* hair.

What you may not know about him: Harry is credited for coming up with the band's name.

Louis William Tomlinson

Birthdate: December 24, 1991
Astrological sign: Capricorn
Hometown: Doncaster, South Yorkshire, England
On Twitter: @Louis_Tomlinson

The basics: Louis, the oldest member of One Direction, says if music hadn't worked out for him, he might have become a drama teacher. Prior to auditioning for *The X*

LOUIS

Factor, Louis' musical experience was limited to a few vocal lessons and the only real stage time he'd seen was in a school production of *Grease.* Fashion-wise, Louis is known for his love of striped shirts.

His rep: He's known both as the group's leader and as its biggest prankster. "Louis is absolutely mental, really off the cuff, but he can also be quite gentle at times," Liam said.

Phone faux pas: Louis made headlines in 2010, when he and fellow band member Harry Styles unwittingly revealed *X-Factor* winner Matt Cardle's personal mobile phone number to 7,000 fans on Twitcam. The boys decided to prank call Matt but it went straight to his voicemail – which read his number out loud. Can you say "oops?"

What you may not know about him: Louis has thoroughly enjoyed his time in the United States but says he misses British food. Now, whenever he travels abroad, he brings along Yorkshire tea so he has a little taste of home nearby.

CHAPTER THREE
WILL U.K. FAME TRANSLATE IN THE U.S.?

The Beatles couldn't do it. Neither could the Rolling Stones or Pink Floyd. When One Direction's first album debuted at No. 1 on the Billboard charts, they did what no other U.K. band had done before.

But it wasn't like others hadn't tried.

Ever since The Tornados' single "Telstar" became the first single by a British band to top the U.S. charts in the early 1960s, conquering the American record-buying market has been the goal of thousands of U.K. musicians. Some have succeeded; many, many others have not.

When it comes to the lack of British acts making it big in America, Keith Causfield, senior chart manager and analyst for *Billboard* magazine, says "size" has everything to do with it.

"In the U.K., a small but dedicated following can have a big impact on the charts," he told NME.com "When Muse first came out,

they were a blip in the U.S. It took *Twilight* (Muse appeared on the soundtrack) to bring them to a whole new audience."

Muse has gone on to enjoy success in the States. Similarly, Americans have shown their love – at least at the cash register – for U.K. acts including Adele, Mumford & Sons, and La Roux.

Music insiders say it's not so much that Americans and Brits have different musical tastes, but rather it's an issue of supply and demand. The U.S. music market is saturated with home-grown bands, making it very difficult for non-American acts to make much of a splash here.

So, how and why has One Direction succeeded in the United States while so many others have failed?

"One Direction is so different from American bands," 15-year-old fan Sydney Durfee told *The (London) Mail* when the group visited Boston in March 2012. "They are polite. And I love their accents."

"I love their hair. They have voices like angels, even though they are just ordinary boys," said Sydney's friend, Jillian Chrisom, also 15.

"They are so sincere," Sydney added. "American boys can be rude, but One Direction is not like that. They are clean and classy."

These girls may speak for the masses.

Take musician Robbie Williams, for example. He's dominated the British charts with

a string of No. 1 hits, but America hasn't exactly fallen in love with him. One reason? How about a 2003 appearance on *The Tonight Show*, when he gyrated on Simon Cowell's knee, rubbed his crotch against

THE BRITISH INVASION

Your parents or grandparents might talk about it, but few folks under the age of 40 have any idea what the British Invasion really was. A quick musical history lesson, if you will:

"British Invasion" is an American term used to describe the many rock and pop performers from the United Kingdom who became popular in the United States during the mid-1960s.

The floodgates were opened when The Beatles arrived in New York City on February 7, 1964. The Beatles' first film, *A Hard Day's Night*, portrayed England as the epicenter of the musical universe. Hungry for fresh sounds, American music lovers bought into the notion.

Within the next two years, at least 10 different U.K. bands and solo artists topped Billboard's singles chart in the United States. Suddenly American teens were singing along to the likes of Manfred Mann's "Do Wah Diddy Diddy," the Troggs' "Wild Thing," and "Mrs. Brown You've Got a Lovely Daughter" by Herman's Hermits. Though groups had distinctly different sounds, it was easy to see that most had been heavily influenced by American rock 'n' roll, blues, and rhythm and blues.

"These charming invaders had borrowed – often literally – American rock music and returned it – restyled and refreshed – to a generation largely ignorant of its historical and racial origins," wrote Ira A. Robbins in *Encyclopedia Britannica Online*.

Many historians and music insiders still wonder how and why the British Invasion happened. The most popular explanation is that it came at the right time and place: following the 1963 assassination of U.S. President John F. Kennedy, Americans yearned for something bright and fun.

Writing in *The Rolling Stone Illustrated History of Rock & Roll*, critic Lester Bangs said British artists of the era produced very little music of enduring importance. "They were, by and large, junk: perfect expressions of the pop aesthetic of a disposable culture."

He concluded, however, that "disposability" was fundamental to the British Invasion's charm: "The central irony of this chapter of rock history is that out of so much worthless music was carved nothing less than the first renaissance of rock 'n' roll."

news woman Katie Couric, and harassed *Austin Powers* actor Mike Myers? His performance of "The Star Bangle Banner" on a late night U.S. talk show, followed by a string of tasteless jokes, also flopped.

Music agent Jonathan Shalit, says Williams' lack of manners and humility simply hasn't played very well in the United States.

"For years, he's got away with this cheeky, chappy image in the U.K., but that just doesn't translate to America," Shalit told *The (London) Daily Mirror.* "He's a massive talent but he's too self-centered and opinionated. He seems to think success should now come to him but if he's really hungry for it, he has to go out there and earn it."

There is a relentless amount of promotion and dedication required to break into the American music scene, and not every artist is prepared to put in the time or effort.

The Parlotones aren't a U.K. band – they're actually from Johannesburg, South

FIVE U.K. ACTS WORTH LISTENING TO

Sure, you know about Adele Leona, Leona Lewis, and Coldplay. Dig a little deeper and you'll find lots of cutting-edge music coming out of the United Kingdom. Here are five acts teetering on the brink of international breakthrough like One Direction. Check them out now and jump on the bandwagon early:

1. **The Wanted.** This British boy band was formed three years ago through a mass audition process. Their breakout single, "Glad You Came," is a danceable blend of world music, hip-hop, and pop, and has received a lot of airplay in the U.S. In recent months, members Max George, Siva Kaneswaran, Jay McGuiness, Tom Parker, and Nathan Sykes, have spent their days touring with heavy hitters including Rihanna, Britney Spears, and Justin Bieber. They're managed by Scooter Braun (Bieber's manager) and have made a splash in the United States in 2012.

2. **Little Mix.** This girl band (formerly known as Rhythmix) became the first group to win *The X Factor* when they walked off with the show's top prize in November 2011. Does this sound familiar? Perrie Edwards, Jesy Nelson, Leigh-Anne Pinnock, and Jade Thirlwall auditioned as soloists and failed to make it past the show's first big challenge. However, judges decided to give them another chance in the Groups category. Initially, they were then put into separate ensembles, but judges pulled these four musicians to form the winning group, sort of like a girls' One Direction. Little Mix's debut single topped the U.K. Singles Chart in December 2011, and made the Christmas 2011 No. 1 spot on the Irish Singles Chart.

3. **Lawson.** This four-piece, London-based band consists of members Andy Brown, Adam Pitts, Joel

5. Flux Pavilion. Joshua Steele, known professionally as Flux Pavilion, is an English electric dance music producer and DJ. He is the co-founder of Circus Records and is best known for his 2011 single "Bass Cannon," which peaked at No. 56 on the U.K. Singles Chart. In December 2011, the British Broadcasting Corporation announced that Flux Pavilion had been nominated for the BBC's Sound of 2012 poll. In early 2012, his track "I Can't Stop" was featured in the viral "KONY 2012" campaign, thus exposing Flux Pavilion to a large new fan base.

Peat, and Ryan Fletcher. The guys met online through MySpace and YouTube, but after a couple of jams and songwriting sessions, they realized these were the friends with whom they wanted to start making music. The band is playing gigs around the U.K. and touring in support of The Wanted. Fun fact: In 2008, neurosurgeon David Lawson performed a life-saving operation on lead singer Andy Brown, removing a brain tumor; the group is named in his honor.

4. Angel. This West London singer/songwriter is responsible for writing Roll Deep's hit "Green Light." He's also written for Jason Derulo, Pixie Lott, and is featured on Wretch 32's Top 5 album *7 Minutes Before Time*. Wretch returned the favor, appearing on Angel's first single, "Go in, Go hard." BBC Radio1 calls him "the new face of U.K. R&B" RWD magazine refers to him as "Britain's answer to Trey Songz and Chris Brown." Angel's debut album premiered in 2012.

Africa – but members agree that trying to break into the U.S. market is a pretty intimidating challenge for any non-U.S. musicians.

"We put off coming to America for quite a while. It's so big. It's daunting," Parolotones guitarist Paul Hodgson told *The Spokesman (Wash.) Review* in March 2011, as his band was embarking on its first U.S. tour. "You can tour the whole U.K. in two weeks, but when you come to America you need at least five weeks."

Fortunately for fans, the One Direction guys and their management have decided that conquering the U.S. is worth the effort. They tour, they show up at mall appearances and book signings, and they answer media questions with smiles on their faces.

"We're just five normal boys from the

U.K. who've been given this opportunity, so we're having a great time working very hard," Harry Styles told the Associated Press in March 2012.

The fans of One Direction have been hard at work, as well. Thanks to social media, the group's followers have helped to spread the word about their music.

"It's played a massive part," Harry said. "Twitter, Facebook, and YouTube have been a large percentage of the reason we've been known outside of the U.K. ... We owe a massive thank you to the fans."

"Whenever you ask anyone how they know about us, it's always Twitter or Tumblr or something like that," Louis Tomlinson added.

Frank Riley, founder of the booking agency High Road Touring, has worked with a handful of U.K. artists on their North American tours. He says industry politics used to play a huge role in who made it and who didn't, but acknowledges that technology has changed all that.

"(Previously) a few people held all the keys to the media—radio, television, print—and those on the inside got the attention," he said. "In the new days you'd think

it would be all about talent, but it's not. There are different politics – but a lot more chaos."

Billboard's Caulfield agreed, saying: "A viral (video) can only take you so far; if you can't build a story around that, you're just an act with a popular video."

Caulfield adds that for some, fame in the United States is neither obtainable nor worth bothering with. He points to U.K. stars Williams, Kylie Minogue, and Cheryl Cole as prime examples.

"When you're that huge and you have a decade-long career behind you, do you even want to try and break America?" he said. "You come here and you're a new artist. Some acts might just prefer to be anonymous."

Rapper and singer Plan B puts himself into that category.

"I worry about becoming successful in America, because I know how much hard work and touring it would be," he told NME.com. "I don't know if I want to break into the U.S. to be honest. I might sell more records but then my films and the stuff I'm passionate about would suffer."

It's not difficult to see why some U.K. bands have a hard time making a go of it stateside. It's a little more bewildering

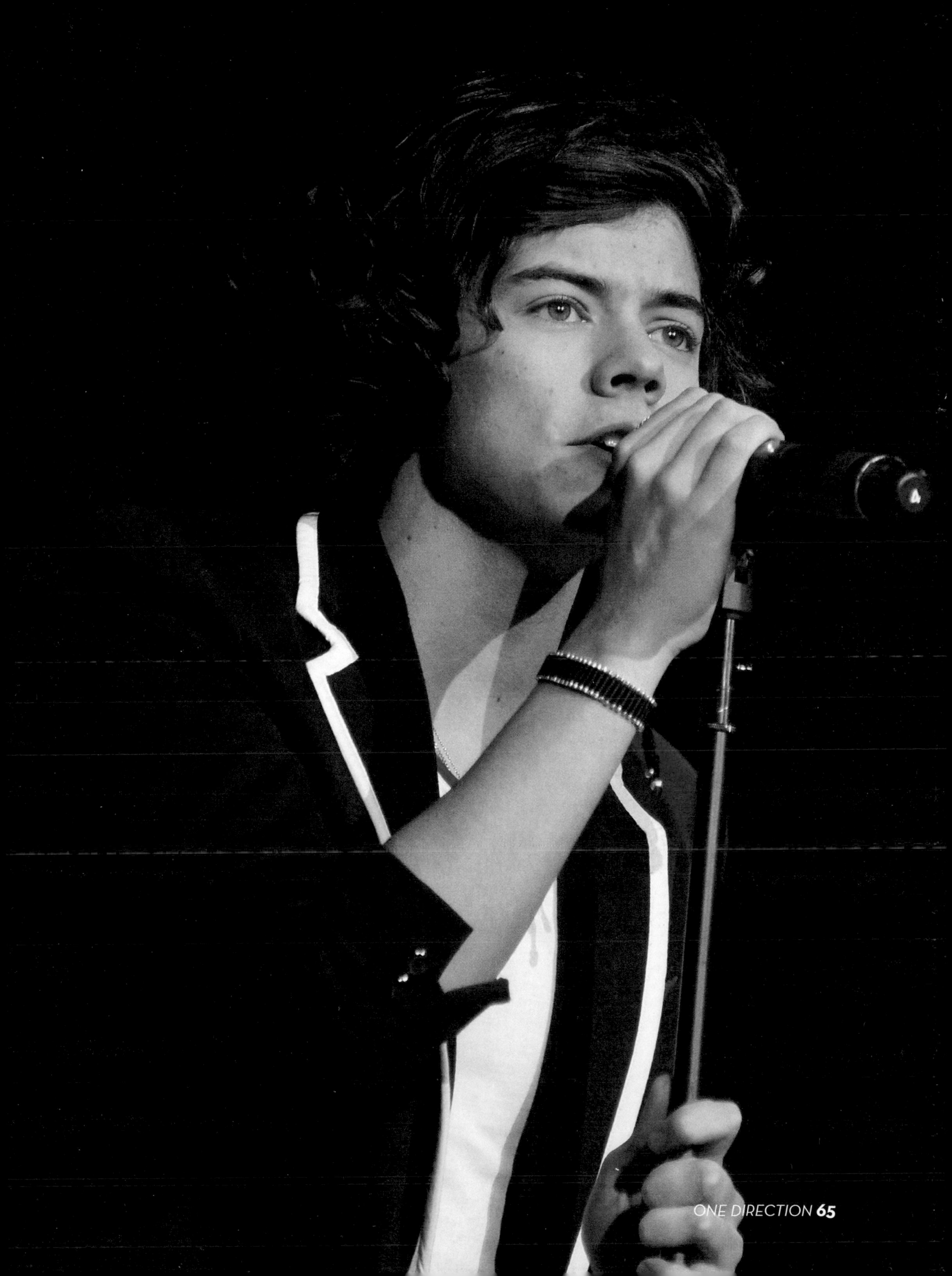

to hear about U.S. bands that are enjoying great success overseas but not getting much airplay in their home country. Nashville, Tenn.-based Mona has done just that. The band's debut album was getting rave reviews in the United Kingdom, a full nine months before it was released in the States.

"It was a Top 40 album in the U.K. and Europe," said Mona vocalist Nick Brown. "We were No. 1 on MTV and stuff like that. It's weird – it's two different worlds. Over there, we exist and over here, it's like we're just starting again."

While no one claims to know the true secret to making it in the U.S. music business, Caulfield suggests the formula might look something like this:

Hit single + Hard work + Popular TV commercials + Talk shows + Touring + A bit of British flair, but not too much = *Possible success*

He may be right. The One Direction guys have most of those factors working in their favor and everything seems to be adding up just fine for them.

CHAPTER FOUR
BOY BANDS

As long as there are teenaged girls, there will be boy bands. It's a fact of life – embrace it. The members of One Direction have and they're not shy about leading the pack in what has become a fairly populated and often criticized musical genre.

"They say it's not a good thing to be in a boy band," One Direction's Liam Payne told HitFix.com in March 2012, acknowledging that the term is "cheesy" and "a little bit of a dirty word."

"We want to change that," he said. "We want to make the boy band cool. It's not just about dancing and dressing the same."

So, lots of bands have only male members. What makes a boy band different? Well, dancing and dressing the same can play into it; many boy bands perform highly choreographed routines. Generally speaking, boy band members don't play musical instruments. In most cases, the groups are

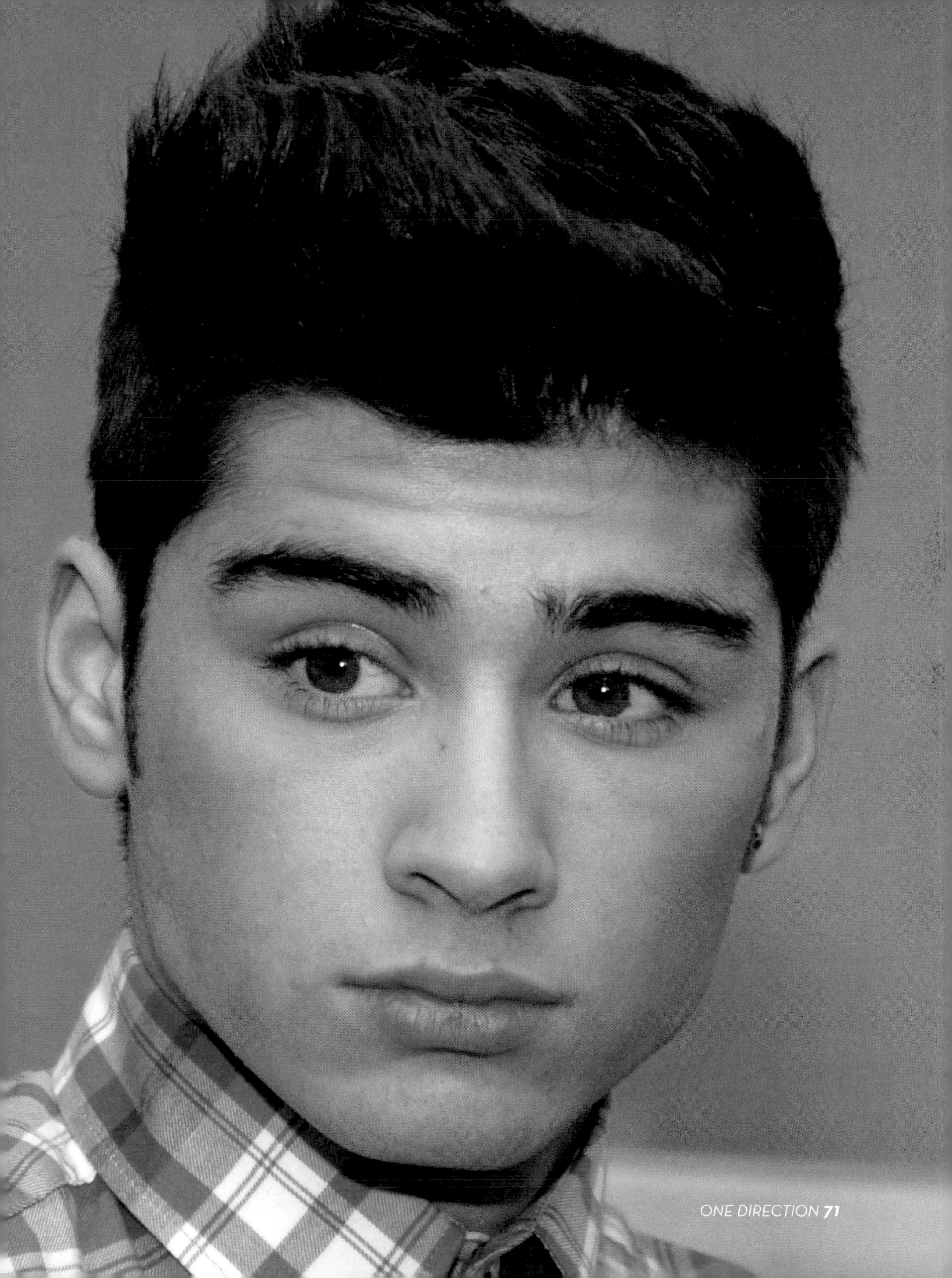

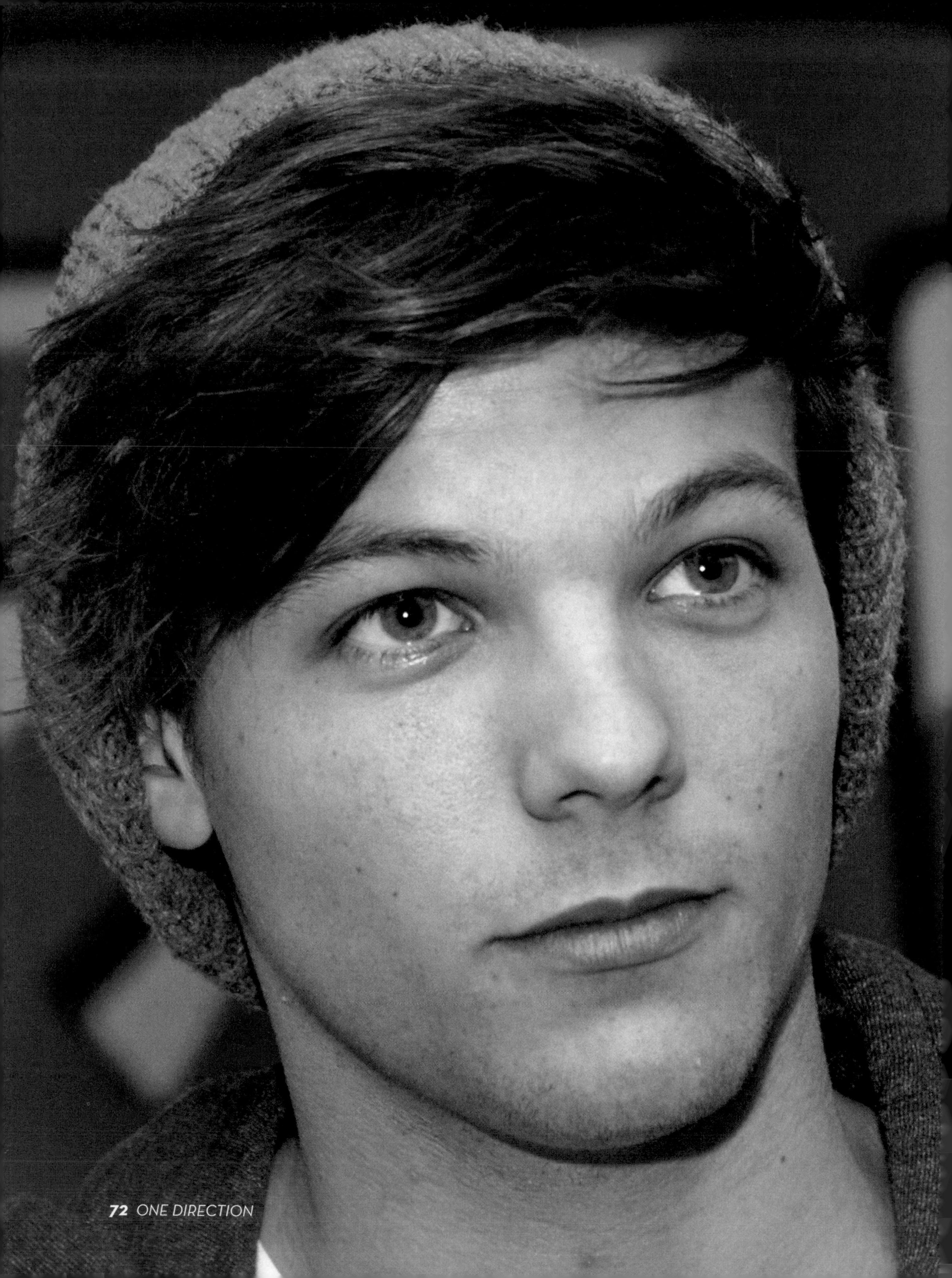

brought together by a producer or through an audition process and they rarely write their own music. The group's image is carefully managed, and often individual band members are portrayed as having a particular personality type (such as One Direction's "sensible" Liam, "flirty" Harry, and "funny" Niall). The performers are almost always good looking.

One Direction already has busted out of at least a couple of the boy band stereotypes: The guys don't dance and they have co-writing credits on three of the songs featured on their debut album, *Up All Night*.

"I think we'd like to do more writing on the next album, but when you've got so many good songs coming at you, you can't turn down a good song," Liam acknowledged.

Boy bands have been around for more than 100 years – even if they weren't originally called "boy bands" (that term didn't come around until the 1980s). The earliest examples were a capella barbershop quartets that sang four-part harmonies. In the 1940s and '50s, rhythm and blues-inspired doo wop groups filled the role.

In the 1960s, all-male groups including

The Osmonds, The Jackson 5, and The Monkees took center stage. This was also the decade when The Beatles set the standard for boy bands to follow in terms of marketing to young women; Beatles novelty merchandise was very popular as were the group's movies.

A-Ha, New Edition, and The Bay City Rollers became teen heartthrobs of the 1970s and '80s. They paved the way for the boy band movement of the 1990s, when groups including New Kids on the Block,

FIVE NOTABLE MUSIC TRENDS

Boy bands are the hot music trend of the moment, but there have been many others throughout the years. Some you should know about:

Song-specific dances. Over the years, many songs have been written and performed to exploit emerging dance crazes or to create new dance styles. "The Loco-Motion" and "Mashed Potato Time" are early examples. In the 1970s and '80s there were "YMCA," "The Hustle,"and "Walk Like An Egyptian." More recently there's been the "Macarena," "The Ketchup Song," and "Cha Cha Slide."

Making it add up. This isn't so much a trend as it is an odd phenomenon. Throughout the years there have been dozens – maybe even hundreds – of top-tier musical acts with numbers in their names. Here are a few for your review: Maroon 5, U2, 3 Dog Night, Ben Folds Five, B-52s, Blink 182, 10,000 Maniacs, Nine-Inch Nails, Matchbox Twenty, and 50 cent. Hmmm ... interesting that One Direction fits right in here, isn't it?

Charitable tunes. "We Are the World" was recorded in 1985 and, all these years later, remains the top charity single of all time. Written by Michael Jackson and Lionel Richie, this emotional ballad raised more than $63 million and featured vocal solos by some of the biggest artists of the time, including Stevie Wonder, Tina Turner, Billy Joel, Willie Nelson, and Bruce Springsteen. Though it's the biggest, there have been many other charitable songs recorded. A few of the most notable are 1984's "Do They Know It's Christmas" with proceeds going to provide relief for famine in Ethiopia; 1985's "That's What Friends Are For" which raised more than $3 million for AIDS research; and, 2005's "Come Together Now," recorded to benefit the victims of Hurricane Katrina and the 2004 Indian Ocean tsunami.

Singing with a Buddy. Collaborations have long been popular but they may have hit a peak in 2011 when anyone who was anyone recorded a blockbuster collaboration. Some pairings you couldn't miss: Christina Aguilera joined Maroon 5 on "Moves Like Jagger;" Pitbull collaborated with Ne-Yo, Afrojack, and Nayer on "Give Me Everything;" Kanye West joined Katy Perry on "ET;" Adam Levine joined Gym Class Heroes on "Stereo Hearts;" and, Justin Bieber and Usher teamed up for "The Christmas Song."

Mobile Music. In recent years, the "access" to music has become an increasingly important trend. Thanks to the iPod, the success of networks like Last.fm and MySpace Music, cloud storage services and streaming audio providers, coupled with the popularity of smart phones and tablets, users now have unprecedented access to libraries of music regardless of location. It's a fundamental shift that will surely change how you are going to listen to music.

Boyz II Men, Backstreet Boys, 'N Sync, 98 Degrees, O-Town, and Dream Street dominated the music scene. The Jonas Brothers were the only boy band of real significance from 2000-2010.

Over the past few years, the U.S. airwaves have been dominated by hip-hop artists. Beginning in late 2011, however, music started morphing into heavy-rhythm pop and then straight pop.

"Acts like Katy Perry and Rihanna have paved the way for pure pop music's return," Keith Caulfield, *Billboard* magazine's associate director of charts, told the Associated Press in March 2012. "What's been missing were girl groups and boy bands. It's such a good environment for this kind of act in pop music right now."

Sharon Dastur, program director for New York City's Z100 (WHTZ 100.3 FM) agrees the environment and timing have been ripe for a boy band resurgence. "Music is always very cyclical," she said. "We had the New-Kids-on-the-Block time and the

THINK YOU WANT TO START YOUR OWN BAND?

You play the guitar. You have friends who sing and play the drums. Maybe you should form a band...

It's that deceptively easy – and difficult – all at the same time.

Before you even start gathering musicians for a band, you need to decide what kind of music you want to play and how serious you intend to be about it. Are you hoping to hit the Billboard charts or do you just want to play at local clubs?

Once you've decided those things, you can start spreading the word through friends, your online social networks, and local music stores. As you hold auditions, take the time to find band mates who can not only play, but who you get along with, as well. You'll end up spending lots of time together, rehearsing and traveling to shows – and you don't want to do that with someone you simply can't stand.

Mark Zonder, drummer for the band Slavior, provides valuable band-forming advice in a 2008 issue of *Modern Drummer* magazine: "Don't be in a hurry ... Getting along on a personal as well as an artistic level is important, because the road you'll share will have its ups and downs ... You're not likely to make the perfect connection right off the bat."

Right off the bat, you and your potential band mates need to make some decisions:
- How often do you plan to practice and where?
- Will everyone have some creative input, or is there only one songwriter?
- If there are band-related expenses, like traveling to shows or renting practice space, now is the time to work out who pays for what. Also, be sure to discuss potential income and how it might be divided.
- Who's the "boss?" Often the songwriter or the person who formed the band takes on leadership responsibilities. You may plan to run the band as a democracy, but when it comes time to book shows or promote the band, you'll need someone to serve as the group's main contact.

Once you've assembled a group of musicians who seem focused on the same goals, you'll want to start playing. Practice like crazy and then practice some more. When you're sure you're ready, start booking some shows. Most groups have to start out playing dances or parties or small shows – it's just part of the natural progression. The more you perform, the more experience you have, the better your resume, and the more likely you are to book shows in larger venues for greater pay.

"Starting your own band can be frustrating – and it's never free of expense, heartache, and obstacles," Zonder said. "But overcoming all that and achieving this goal will leave you with a unique and amazing sense of accomplishment and pride."

'N Sync-Backstreet Boys time, and now it's that time again."

So, after a decade during which boy bands were fairly scarce, they're back – with a vengeance.

The One Direction guys currently are sharing the music spotlight with a handful of other all-male groups:

•U.K.-based The Wanted's single "Glad You Came" became a hit in the United States in March 2012. The band opened several shows for Justin Bieber and Britney Spears in 2011 and did a two-month U.S. tour in early 2012. The Wanted puts a twist on the genre's generally wholesome image: Its lyrics are laced with references to partying and sexual hookups.

•Big Time Rush is a four-member boy

band that also has a hit Nickelodeon show. The group wrapped a sold-out U.S. tour (featuring One Direction as the opening act) at New York's Radio City Music Hall in March 2012 and had a larger North American tour in the summer of 2012.

•Mindless Behavior debuted at No. 2 on the R&B charts in late 2010 with its album *#1 Girl*. The band was formed by Keisha Gamble, Walter Milsap (who previously worked with Beyonce and Timbaland), and Vincent Herbert (the same guy who discovered Lady Gaga.) The four-member group quickly moved from touring high schools to opening sold-out tours for the Backstreet Boys, Janet Jackson, and Justin Bieber.

•Anthem Lights, originally known as Yellow Cavalier, is a high-energy pop foursome with a Christian music bent. The group released a self-titled album (their first on Reunion Records and the first under their current name) in May 2011. They've toured nationally with Building 429,

MercyMe, Jars of Clay, and The Afters.

"(The boy band phenomenon) is just exploding," Radio Disney on-air-personality Ernie D. told the Associated Press. "It's

BOY BAND ALUMNUS JUSTIN TIMBERLAKE

In the 1980s and '90s, the airwaves were dominated by the pop stylings of 'N Sync, Backstreet Boys, 98 Degrees, O-Town, and Five. But where, oh where, have these heart-throbs gone?

'N Sync's J.C. Chasez's 2004 solo debut, *Schizophrenic*, sold respectably and he's gone on to write and produce for acts Girls Aloud, Basement Jaxx, David Archuleta, Matthew Morrison, and the Backstreet Boys.

Nick Lachey, who performed with 98 Degrees, has enjoyed lackluster sales of his solo projects but has become something of a celebrity thanks to TV appearances on *Charmed, One Tree Hill* and as host of *The Sing Off.*

It's true, a handful of boy band alumni have found success on stage or in front of the camera, but the only certified star to have emerged from that era is Justin Timberlake.

Timberlake is one of the few artists who have been able to make the leap from teen heartthrob to serious, adult artist. He's traded in his image as a wholesome teen singer for that of a hottie on the prowl; in recent years he's had very public romances with starlets Cameron Diaz, Alyssa Milano, and is engaged to actress Jessica Biel.

He's also convinced the record-buying public that his talents go far beyond dancing and looking handsome alongside a couple other guys. He's a gritty, soulful singer whose first two solo albums made him one of the world's most commercially successful singers with sales of more than 7 million copies. "SexyBack" became Timberlake's first No. 1 single on the Billboard Hot 100, staying seven weeks at the top spot in 2006.

He's won six Grammy Awards, two Emmy Awards, and has, in recent years, spent more time on the big screen than on the concert stage. His latest films include *The Social Network, Bad Teacher* and *Friends with Benefits.*

Justin Timberlake is one boy band alumnus who isn't going quietly into the night.

really amazing to see, especially on my end, hearing all the calls from the listeners. ... So, that fever is definitely growing for sure."

As the fever grows, acceptance of the "boy band" label also appears to increase.

Big Time Rush members admit they weren't at all excited about being called a boy band when they debuted in late 2009.

"We hated that term to start with," James Maslow said.

"Because the term hadn't come back yet," continued band mate Kendall Schmidt. "We kind of feel like we paved the way for it to come back."

At first glance, it might seem that having multiple boy bands enter the U.S. market at the same time would hurt all their chances of success. In fact, just the opposite seems

to be happening. Fans reason that if they enjoy the sound of One Direction, they might also enjoy music by another U.K. boy band – they sample, they enjoy, and their musical repertoires are broadened. Similarly, having other bands perform the same sort of music forces each group to push a little harder to distinguish themselves from the crowd.

"It's giving us that little competition that makes us want to go further and excel further than we are right now," Big Time Rush's Carlos Pena Jr. said.

Maslow added: "We want to support other boy bands as well because we really want that whole genre to come back."

If chart-topping singles and sold-out arenas are any indication, Big Time Rush, One Direction, The Wanted, and others have proven that boy bands have made a very big comeback in 2012. How long this particular surge in their popularity will last is impossible to predict but, for now, it's certain that the girls who love boys who sing are very, very happy.

CHAPTER FIVE
FANtastic

You adore the way your musical idols harmonize. You love their hair, their clothes, their good manners, and British charm. You are a Directioner.

And, as crazy as you are about One Direction, you know you're not alone. The boys in this band have quickly gathered a large, enthusiastic, and ear-splittingly loud army of fans.

It's "Biebermania multiplied by five," suggested *(London) Daily Mail* writer Leah McDonald. It's true: "One Direction Infection" is spreading around the world at record pace.

During a March 2012 visit to New York City, band member Louis Tomlinson thought it would be funny to press his hands up against the back window of the group's bus. He teased the screaming girls running behind it, yelling: "Come on then, get it!"

What he hadn't counted on was the fact

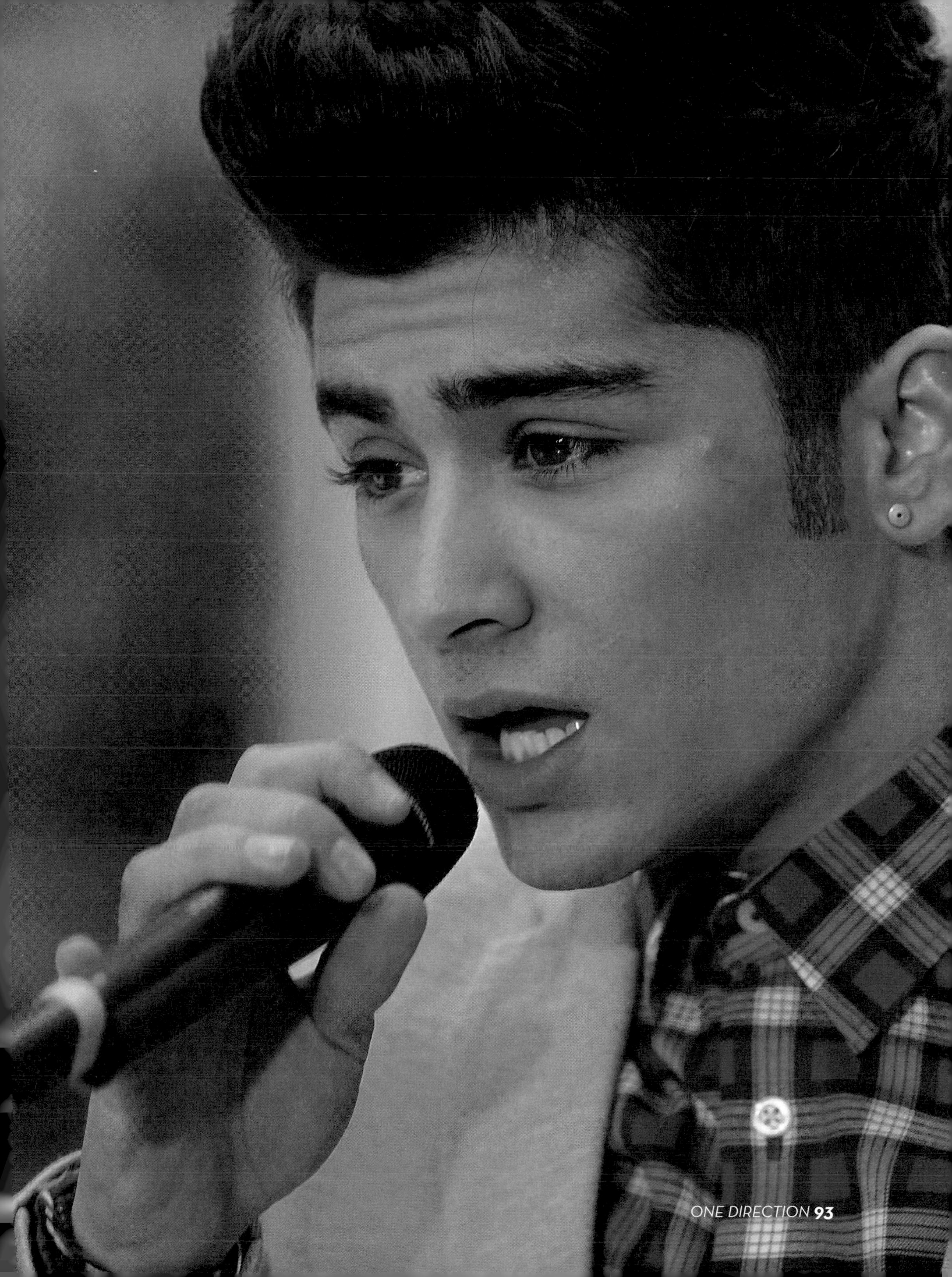

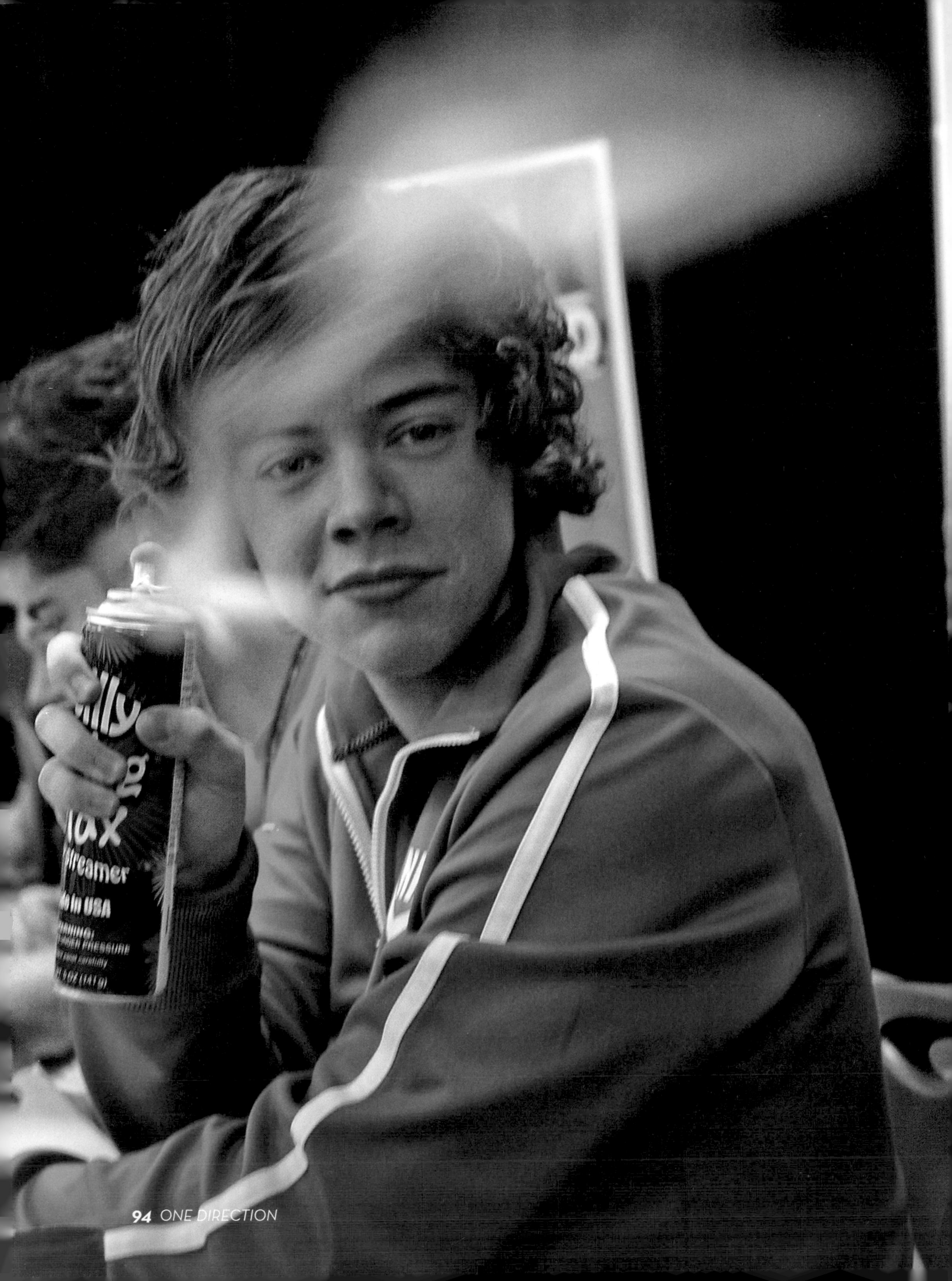

that the street light would turn red, the bus would be forced to stop, and the overzealous mob would catch up to the vehicle, banging on its windows and rocking it from side to side.

After a few scary moments, the bus was able to get moving again, leaving the hysterical mob in its wake.

Fans around the world adore Niall, Zayn, Liam, Harry, and Louis, but U.S. fans seem to be among the most rabid.

"The fans over here are really loud and crazy," Niall Horan told *The (London) Mirror*. "When we're in the tour bus, they start climbing all over it and smacking on the windows, trying to get in. They start chasing after us, screaming."

The band has received similar receptions as they've traveled across the United States:

- When they performed live for the first time on American television in early March 2012, a crowd of 10,000 prompted NBC's *Today* show to call in extra security.
- In Nashville, dozens of girls chased the band's car through the streets of Music Row.
- In Natick, Mass., 5,000 fans mobbed a

mall when the members of One Direction held an autograph signing there.

- A security team of 100 was assigned to protect the group for their 45-minute show at Dallas' Dr. Pepper Park on March 25.

A number of critics and music insiders have likened fans' reaction to One Direction to that of The Beatles, when they first came to the states in 1964. Of course, the 1D guys weren't around when that happened, but they've seen footage and they

FANS SET SIGHTS ON FAN SITES

One Direction and its record company have put together an excellent website packed with information about appearances, music, photos, online newsletter, ticket sales, and more. (Check it out at www.onedirectionmusic.com.)

But, let's face it, sometimes one website simply can't provide all the information you crave. Thank goodness for fan sites.

These unofficial sites are created by fans for fans. Their sole purpose is to let One Directioners come together to read about their band, look at photos, and express their passion for the guys. There are dozens of One Direction fan sites out there, a few of our favorites include:

OneDirectionFans.Net

This well-designed fan site was launched Jan. 1, 2012, and includes links to TV appearances, tweets, photos, news clips, tour dates, lyrics, and more. In its first three months of existence, the site's photo gallery attracted more than 1 million unique views. It's clear the site's web princess puts a lot of effort into this project; it's an excellent, up-to-date place to go for info about the band.

Onedirectionfans.org

This was established in October 2011 and re-opened in 2012 with a new look and feel that promises daily news and the addition of thousands of new photos and icons. We like the site's video of the week feature and the chat box that allows fans to interact.

Onedirectiononline.com

Established in March 2011, this site bills itself as the "first U.S. fansite for One Direction" and has attracted 1.4 million hits in its first 12 months online. The site includes tour dates, lots of terrific photos, song clips, media clips, tweets, a message board, and fan fiction. It's a well organized site packed with the sort of essentials a fan is looking for.

One-direction.fan-sites.org

This fan site isn't quite as jam-packed with information as some of the others, but it showcases some really terrific photos. You'll find short bios on the band members, as well as information about appearances, signings, performances, and more. The site was set up in October 2011 and is definitely worth checking out.

Onedirectionfanclub.co.U.K.

This site bills itself as a "fan network." It's sort of an online fan club that allows members (it's free to sign up but you must be 13 or older) to create profiles, share videos and photos, and connect with other fans. You can even have your own blog dedicated to One Direction – the site features one dedicated fan each month. Thanks to the sharing of information, the site posts about 450 video clips and more than 7,800 photos.

can identify with the pandemonium.

"To be compared to something that was so big in its day is amazing," Louis said. "To be our generation's Beatles ... Wow. It is hugely flattering, but I'm not sure how seriously we can take it because it seems so unrealistic."

Mark Medina, program director at the Washington, D.C., radio station Hot 99.5 says he's seen dozens of pop sensations come and go, but the reception One Direction is getting has astonished him.

When the group played at his station in early March 2012, fans arrived – with signs in hand – a full eight days before the guys' scheduled appearance. At least four girls in the crowd flew across the country, from San Diego, to hear the band play two songs and get a photo.

"I'd never seen anything like it," he told the *Washington Post*. "We had people fly in from other states; we had girls trying to sneak into the building."

It's the kind of devotion with which

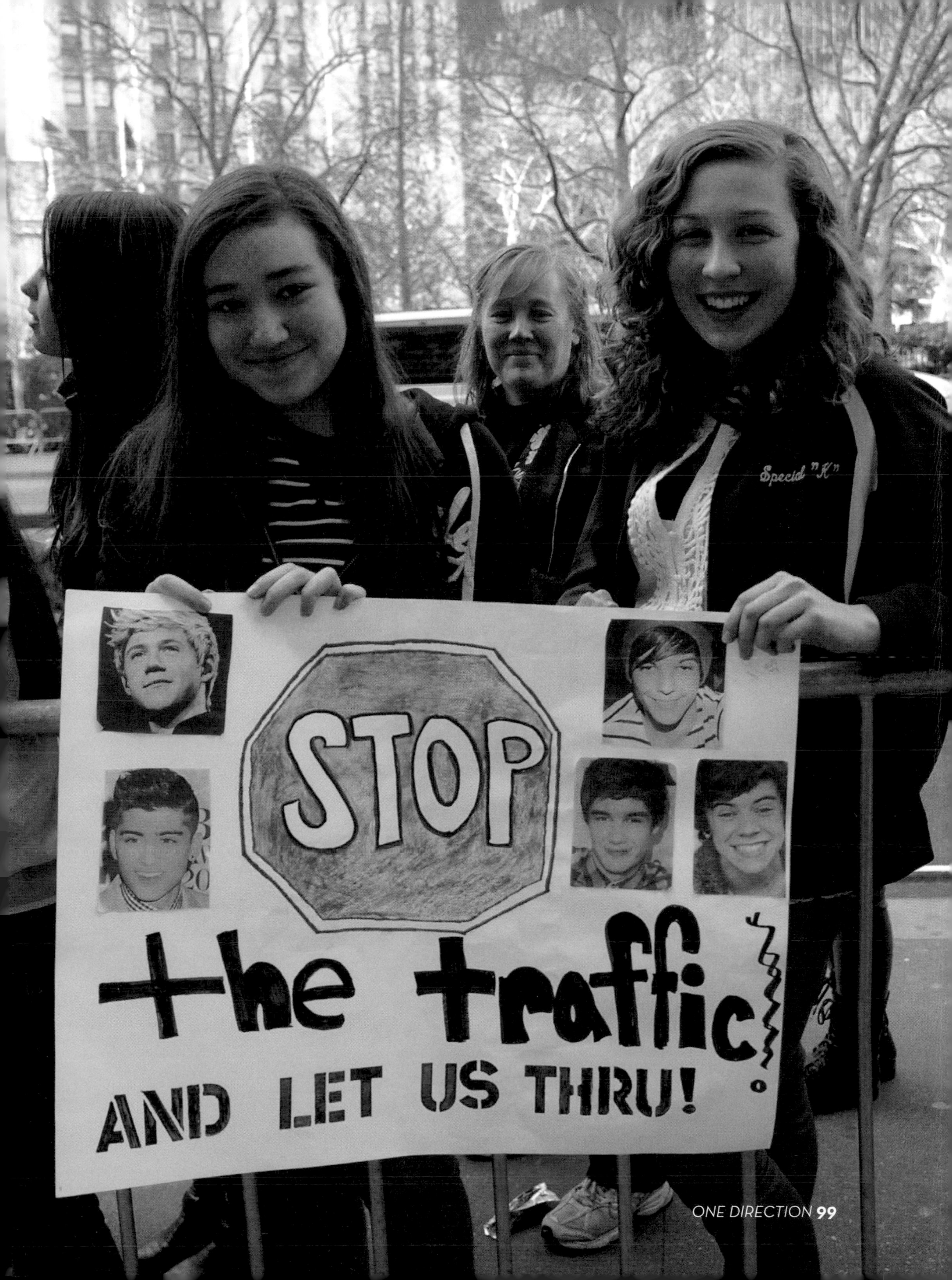
Special "K"
STOP
the traffic!
AND LET US THRU!

MEGA MERCHANDISE

You've always longed to hold Niall, Zayn, Liam, Harry, and Louis in your arms – and now you can. Well, not them exactly, but doll-sized versions of the pop stars.

Toymaker Vivid Imaginations put out a line of One Direction dolls – make that action figures – in time for Christmas 2011. The collectible dolls, which measure about 13 inches tall and cost $27 to $43 each, are outfitted to look just like the real thing: Harry, for example, is posed in a button-down shirt, sweater, and jacket while the Zayn doll is wearing a jacket with the One Direction logo. If one boy band member just isn't enough, fans can collect the whole gang and relive the excitement of one of their high-energy concerts. The guys confided to *People* magazine that they sent creator Simon Cowell a set of the dolls as a cheeky thank-you gift.

Dolls aren't your thing? Fear not! One Direction has a wide variety of merchandise available.

The guys can go to school with you if you invest in a One Direction lunch box or backpack. You'd rather take them to the pool? You can do that, thanks to the One Direction beach towel.

Perhaps you'd prefer to decorate your room with One Direction posters, stickers, and door hangers?

The boys' handsome images are also available on water bottle covers, tote bags, T-shirts, hoodies, coffee mugs, key rings, bracelets, earrings, pendants, phone cases, DVDs, and so much more.

While it seems the One Direction guys have done just fine in the merchandising department, they have a long way to go before they find themselves listed among artists with the most unusual merchandise.

The A.V. Club, for example, has a coloring book among its offerings. Metallica sells metal light switch plates. And perhaps the oddest merchandise of all, the rock band KISS, known for its face paint and flamboyant stage outfits, sells a coffin decorated with pictures of the band. The "Kiss Kasket" is available through the band's website for $3,299 plus shipping.

A coffin? Thanks, but no thanks. We'll just stick with a One Direction T-shirt (and dolls – er, action figures – of course!)

15-year-old Harleigh Nunez is familiar. She and her mom, Susan, traveled seven hours from Louisiana for One Direction's general admission Dallas show.

"This is a once-in-a-lifetime thing to have this experience," Harleigh told the local NBC television affiliate, adding that she follows the band on Twitter and has a wall of pictures at home in their honor.

"I have four copies of their album," she said. "My computer has a folder that's just full of pictures."

The fan-tastic fan tales continue – at an autograph session in Long Island a fan touched Zayn's hand and then fainted.

"That was probably the weirdest thing I've ever experienced. I've seen girls fainting in crowds and stuff, like when we were

performing, but I'd never seen anything like it that close. She just completely fainted, like, passed out on the floor," he told *USA Today.*

Each day the group receives deliveries of flowers, chocolates, proposals of marriage, and underwear – yes, underwear – from admiring fans. They've also collected stacks and stacks of cards and letters, many of which are decorated with flowers and smiley faces and lots of tiny hearts.

Even the boys' mothers aren't safe from the rush of fans. At the group's Boston show in March 2012, Niall Horan's mom, Maura, was swamped by fans anxious to be photographed with her.

Fans are drawn to the group for a variety of reasons: the boys' good looks, their accents, their graciousness, their girl-centric lyrics.

No matter the specific attraction, most fans seem to react in the same way: They scream with an intensity that's actually painful to endure.

"They're very loud," Zayn Malik told the *Today* show when asked about American girls.

That may actually be a bit of an

understatement. A member of One Direction's management team tells *The Guardian* he's seen recordings that show the screaming has reached 104 decibels – that's louder than a jet at take off and a level at which sustained exposure can cause hearing loss.

Even if they can't hear what's being shrieked at them, the guys say they especially love it when fans show up at concerts wearing handmade T-shirts or carrying posters and banners. Those are the sorts of personal touches that show a genuine

effort to connect with the band.

"In Boston we did a meet-and-greet and these five girls came dressed as each of us," Harry Styles told *The (London) Mirror*. "They do that a lot. It's cool."

And, so, the guys must be particularly pleased with fans like 16-year-old Katelyn Conlon who attended their Boston show wearing a shirt she'd decorated with neon carrots. ... "Carrots?" you ask.

In a 2010 video diary for the *The X Factor's* web site, Louis revealed that he likes girls who like carrots.

It's those special touches, those indications that the fans in the crowd are the same people who are listening to their music and reading their tweets, and watching their behind-the-scenes videos that make the guys feel loved.

"It's a massive cliché but it's 100 percent the stuff of dreams, an unbelievable feeling," Harry Styles told the *(London) Daily Mirror*. "We're five normal lads given this massive opportunity and know that without the fans we'd be nowhere. We feel incredibly grateful."

EPILOGUE

Things are happening so fast for One Direction that it's hard to tell exactly how high their star will climb. What is certain, however, is that the group's immediate future looks very, very bright.

The guys' CD is flying off the shelves, they're getting tons of radio play, their photos are on the covers of dozens of magazines, and the announcement of their first North American tour saw young fans busting open their piggy banks for ticket-buying money.

Like many new musical acts, the guys in One Direction have been steered through these early phases of stardom by experienced managers who tell them where to go, what to wear, when to eat and sleep, what to say to the media, who to work with, even how many autographs to sign before they have to get on the bus. Liam Payne said giving up that kind of control isn't difficult, especially because the guys place so much faith in their advisors.

"Thankfully, we got lots of say in the album, actually," Liam told *The Irish Times*. "We got to choose a lot of the songs and that sort of stuff. That was important to us with *X Factor*, too – we kind of put our own stamp on the boy band thing."

The guys are proud that they got assists on their debut album from songwriting and production big-wigs including Savan Kotecha, RedOne, and Kelly Clarkson. They're even prouder that they were able to share in the songwriting duties on a few of the album's songs.

"Some of the time we actually sat there and there was no song – we came up with the concept from the beginning," Liam said. "Toby Gad was one of the guys we wrote with. He wrote 'If I Were a Boy,' which was obviously a massive song – so to work with someone like that when we're just starting off is a massive deal."

It was a big deal, but the guys insist they were comfortable with it.

"Songwriting's a very precious thing, you know," said Zayn Malik. "When you write your own music you can be quite precious about it, and it can be quite hard to express it to people. But we always felt comfortable. And we had each other to show our ideas to."

As successful as 1D's first album has been, it's doubtful their second CD – which is already in development – will stray too far artistically.

Niall Horan told the *National Post* that the group is already meeting with songwriters and producers, with the goal of heading into the studio this in summer 2012.

"We want to bring out a record nearly every year, every year and a half," he said.

The guys promise future projects will reflect their own, personal music tastes. Niall, for example, prefers The Script and singer-songwriter Ed Sheeran. Harry's musical tastes lean toward Foster the People, Coldplay, and Kings of Leon.

"We want to have a little bit heavier guitars, bigger drums, more of a live feel, because that's what we like doing," said Harry, insisting fans shouldn't worry about the group moving away from its pop roots and into the grunge scene.

WHAT DOES THE FUTURE HOLD?

"...It's important that we like what we're doing as well," Harry said. "It wouldn't be good if we weren't enjoying what we're doing – and we are."

The guys haven't ruled out collaborating with other artists and, in fact, have mentioned Paul McCartney and Big Time Rush as acts they'd love to perform with. At the same time, Justin Bieber's manager, Scooter Braun suggests JB and 1D might well team up in the near future. When a fan asked about such a pairing during a live question-and-answer session on Twitter, Braun tweeted: *"Very possible. He likes them and thinks they are good dudes. All people of that generation should be there to help each other."*

While music, of course, is the group's main focus, they've released their own calendar and behind-the-scenes book, and they starred in their own road movie, a British documentary that charted their path to pop stardom. They've also made a handful of appearances on U.S. television.

One Direction has guest started on *iCarly* and they've been the musical guests on *Saturday Night Live*, but it's unclear – at least for now – how much more screen time the guys will be getting.

Shortly after One Direction and Big Time Rush attended the 2012 Nickelodeon Upfront presentation in New York City on March 14, the honchos at Nick announced that Niall, Zayn, Liam, Harry, and Louis would be teaming up with the top kids network for future projects. They tweeted: *"The rumors are true, our live-action slate does include a development project for* @onedirection. *Welcome to the family!"*

Now, however, it appears the announcement was a little premature.

Louis Tomlinson told InDemand.com on March 21: "I think there must have been some kind of misunderstanding there. We are doing the Nickelodeon Kids Choice Awards, but as far as a TV show goes we haven't sat down and had that conversation. And to be honest, if it was up to me personally, I just want to focus on the music for now."

One Directioner Niall Horan echoed Louis' sentiment: "It's nothing that I know about. There's no sign of a TV show in the pipeline."

Television show or not, the guys will be plenty busy. If their international tour is any indication (they've already sold out seven dates at London's O2 arena as part of a 2013 tour of the U.K.), 1D's U.S. shows should be filled-to-the-brim with fans.

Louis Tomlinson says playing to sold-out arenas is one of the best parts of the group's newfound fame.

"Performing is just incredible, when you get out of that stage and you take a moment to realize that some of the banners there are for you," he told *USA Today*. "It's your name on the banner, and they're shouting your name when you sing. That's still so surreal, but amazing."

Louis' other favorite aspect of fame?

"...It's really nice to make my mum proud," he said. "Growing up, when I was at school, I was always talkative in class, didn't do enough work – one of those kids. Now, she can go, 'Oh, you're doing good.'"

Oh, yes, Louis ... you and the guys are doing just fine!